KEEPSAKES

GARDENS

CHARTWELL BOOKS
A division of Book Sales, Inc.
POST OFFICE BOX 7100
114 Northfield Avenue
Edison, N.J. 08818-7100

CLB 4395
© 1995 CLB Publishing, Godalming, Surrey, U.K.

All rights reserved
Manufactured in China
ISBN 0-7858-0299-1

KEEPSAKES

GARDENS

Compiled by
Kenneth Deare

CHARTWELL
BOOKS, INC.

A Delightful Occupation

 I HAVE OFTEN thought that if heaven had given me choice of my position and calling, it should have been on a rich spot of earth, well watered, and near a good market for the productions of the garden. No occupation is so delightful to me as the culture of the earth, and no culture comparable to that of the garden. Such a variety of subjects, some one always coming to perfection, the failure of one thing repaired by the success of another, and instead of one harvest a continued one through the year. Under a total want of demand except for our family table, I am still devoted to the garden. But though an old man, I am but a young gardener.

THOMAS JEFFERSON

FATHERS, INSTIL INTO your children the garden-mania. They will grow up the better for it. Let other arts be only studied to heighten the beauty of the one I advocate. Engaged in planning how to shade a glen, or in contriving how to divert the course of a stream, one is too busy ever to become a dangerous citizen, an intriguing general, or a caballing courtier.

PRINCE DE LIGNE

The Garden

What wondrous life is this I lead!
    Ripe apples drop about my head;
The luscious clusters of the vine
    Upon my mouth do crush their wine;
The nectarine and curious peach
    Into my hands themselves do reach;
Stumbling on melons, as I pass,
    Ensnared with flowers, I fall on grass.

Here at the fountain's sliding foot
    Or at some fruit-tree's mossy root,
Casting the body's vest aside
    My soul into the boughs does glide....

Such was the happy Garden-state
    While man there walked without a mate:
After a place so pure and sweet,
    What other help could yet be meet!
But 'twas beyond a mortal's share
    To wander solitary there:
Two paradises 'twere in one,
    To live in Paradise alone.

ANDREW MARVELL

Maiorana.

The Vegetable Creation

TURNING OUR EYES to the vegetable creation, we find nothing there so beautiful as flowers; but flowers are of almost every sort of shape, and of every sort of disposition; they are turned and fashioned into an infinite variety of forms; and from these forms botanists have given them their names, which are almost as various. What proportions do we discover between the stalks and the leaves of flowers, or between the leaves and pistils?

How does the slender stalk of the rose agree with the bulky head under which it bends? But the rose is a beautiful flower; and can we undertake to say that it does not owe a great deal of its beauty even to that disproportion; the rose is a large flower, yet it grows upon a small shrub: the flower of the apple is very small and grows upon a large tree; yet the rose and the apple blossom are both beautiful, and the plants that bear them are most engagingly attired, notwithstanding this disproportion.

EDMUND BURKE

Bower of Bliss

And over him, art striving to compare
   With nature, did an arbour green dispred,
Framed of wanton ivy, flowering fair,
   Through which the fragrant Eglantine did spread
His pricking arms, entrailed with roses red,
   Which dainty odours round about them threw,
And all within with flowers was garnished,
   That when mild Zephyrus amongst them blew,
Did breathe out bounteous smells, and painted colours show.

And fast beside, there trickled softly down
   A gentle stream, whose murmuring wave did play
Amongst the pumy stones, and made a sound,
   To lull him soft asleep, that by it lay;
The weary traveller, wandering that way,
   Therein did often quench his thirsty heat,
And then by it his weary limbs display,
   While creeping slumber made him to forget
His former pain, and wiped away his toilsome sweat.

EDMUND SPENSER

The Loquacious Lily

'**O** TIGER-LILY,' said Alice, addressing herself to one that was waving gracefully about in the wind, 'I *wish* you could talk!'

'We *can* talk,' said the Tiger-lily, 'when there's anybody worth talking to.'

Alice was so astonished that she couldn't speak for a minute: it quite seemed to take her breath away. At length, as the Tiger-lily only went on waving about, she spoke again, in a timid voice – almost in a whisper. 'And can *all* the flowers talk?'

'As well as *you* can,' said the Tiger-lily. 'And a great deal louder.'

'It isn't manners for us to begin, you know,' said the Rose, 'and I really was wondering when you'd speak! Said I to myself, "Her face has got *some* sense in it, though it's not a clever one!" Still, you're the right colour, and that goes a long way.'

'I don't care about the colour,' the Tiger-lily remarked. 'If only her petals curled up a little more, she'd be all right.'

LEWIS CARROLL

Fruits of the Earth

My garden filled with fruits you may behold,
    And grapes in clusters, imitating gold,
Some blushing bunches of a purple hue,
    And these, and those, are all reserved for you.
Red strawberries, in shades, expecting stand,
    Proud to be gathered by so white a hand.
Autumnal cornels later fruit provide
    And plums, to tempt you, turn their glossy side:
Not those of common kinds, but such alone
    As in Phaeacian orchards might have grown.
Nor chestnuts shall be wanting to your food,
    Nor garden fruits, nor wildings of the wood;
The laden boughs for you alone shall bear;
    And yours shall be the product of the year.

OVID *translated by John Dryden*

I have a garden of my own,
    Shining with flowers of every hue;
I loved it dearly while alone,
    But! I shall love it more with you.

THOMAS MOORE

Advice on Planning

OR THE SIDE GROUNDS, you are to fill them with variety of alleys, private, to give a full shade; some of them, wheresoever the sun be. You are to frame some of them likewise for shelter, that when the wind blows sharp, you may walk as in a gallery: and those alleys must be likewise hedged at both ends, to keep out the wind; and these closer alleys must be ever finely gravelled, and no grass, because of *going* wet. In many of these alleys, likewise, you are to set fruit-trees of all sorts, as well upon the walls as in ranges; and this should be generally observed, that the borders wherein you plant your fruit-trees be fair, and large, and low, and not steep; and set with fine flowers, but thin and sparingly, lest they deceive the trees. At the end of both the side grounds I would have a mount of some pretty height, leaving the wall of the enclosure breast-high, to look abroad into the fields.

FRANCIS BACON

Garden Lore

Every child who has gardening tools,
Should learn by heart these gardening rules:

He who owns a gardening spade,
Should be able to dig the depth of its blade.

He who owns a gardening rake,
Should know what to leave and what to take.

He who owns a gardening hoe,
Must be sure how he means his strokes to go.

But he who owns a gardening fork,
May make it do all the other tools' work

Though to shift, or to pot, or annex what you can,
A trowel's the tool for child, woman, or man.

'Twas the bird that sits in the medlar-tree,
Who sang these gardening saws to me.

JULIANA HORATIA EWING

The Oriental Garden

 WHEREAS THE JOY of the European garden lies in its abundance, the gardens of the Far East are delicate, spare, and made in such a way as to seem not to be made, but grown out of the surrounding landscape. Indeed, they often are such landscape in miniature, the carefully placed rocks and plants an echo of the larger world about them. And for the oriental, each stone, each blossom, every bamboo stem or lotus leaf, the ancient pond, has its spiritual resonance, each thus and so because they are thus and so. Much of the great body of Chinese and Japanese poetry springs from this feeling for the natural world, each aspect of its unchanging change being an aspect of that enlightened way of simply *being* which is the ultimate Way of the truly enlightened man.

LAO YANG

A EUROPEAN WILL scarcely conceive my meaning when I say there is scarce a garden in China which does not contain some fine moral, couched under the general design, where one is not taught wisdom as he walks, and feels the force of some noble truth, or delicate precept, resulting from the disposition of the groves, streams, or grottoes.

OLIVER GOLDSMITH

The Lime-Tree Bower

A delight comes sudden on my heart, and I am glad
    As I myself were there! Nor in this bower,
This little lime-tree bower, have I not mark'd
    Much that has sooth'd me. Pale beneath the blaze
Hung the transparent foliage; and I watch'd
    Some broad and sunny leaf, and lov'd to see
The shadow of the leaf and stem above
    Dappling its sunshine! And that walnut-tree
Was richly ting'd, and a deep radiance lay
    Full on the ancient ivy, which usurps
Those fronting elms, and now, with blackest mass
    Makes their dark branches gleam a lighter hue
Through the late twilight: and though now the bat
    Wheels silent by, and not a swallow twitters,
Yet still the solitary humble-bee
    Sings in the bean-flower! Henceforth I shall know
That Nature ne'er deserts the wise and pure;
    No plot so narrow, be but Nature there,
No waste so vacant, but may well employ
    Each faculty of sense, and keep the heart
Awake to Love and Beauty!

SAMUEL TAYLOR COLERIDGE

Glories of the Orchard

HAT CAN YOUR EYE desire to see, your ears to hear, your mouth to take, or your nose to smell, that is not to be had in an orchard, with abundance of variety? What more delightsome than an infinite variety of sweet smelling flowers, decking with sundry colours the green mantle of the earth, the universal mother of us all. Behold in diverse corners of your orchard, earth covered with fruit trees, Kentish cherries, Damsons, plums, etc, and in some corner (or more) a true dial or clock. Large walks, broad and long, close and open, like the Temple groves in Thessaly, raised with gravel and sand, having seats and banks of camomile; all this delights the mind and brings health to the body. View now with delight the works of your own hands, your fruit trees of all sorts, loaden with sweet blossoms, and fruit of all tastes, operations, and colours: your trees standing in comely order, which way soever you look. Your border on every side hanging and dropping with raspberries, barberries, currants, and the roots of your trees powdered with strawberries, red, white and green; what a pleasure this is!

Orchard, it shall be a pleasure to have a bowling alley, or rather (which is more manly, and more healthful) a pair of buts [an archery range], to stretch your arms.

WILLIAM LAWSON

King Jesus's Garden

King Jesus hath a garden full of divers flow'rs,
  Where I go culling posies gay, all times and hours.
There naught is heard but paradise bird,
  Harp, dulcimer, lute,
With cymbal, trump and tymbal,
  And the tender soothing flute;
With cymbal, trump and tymbal,
  And the tender soothing flute.

The lily, white in blossom there is chastity,
  The violet with sweet perfume, humility.
There naught is heard but paradise bird,
  Harp, dulcimer, lute, etc.

Ah! Jesus Lord, my heal and weal, my bliss complete.
  Make thou my heart thy garden-plot, fair, trim and neat.
That I may hear this music clear:
  Harp, dulcimer, lute,
With cymbal, trump and tymbal,
  And the tender soothing flute;
With cymbal, trump and tymbal,
  And the tender soothing flute.

TRADITIONAL DUTCH CAROL
English translation by G. R. Woodward

A Tangle of Flowers

O N THE OTHER SIDE of the drive there was a high box border and the paths had box edges and all of them led into a deeper and deeper tangle of flowers. The camellias were in bloom, white and crimson and pink and white striped with flashing leaves. You could not see a leaf on the syringa bushes for the white clusters. The roses were in flower – gentlemen's button-hole roses, little white ones, but far too full of insects to hold under anyone's nose, pink monthly roses with a ring of fallen petals round the bushes, cabbage roses on thick stalks, moss roses, always in bud, pink smooth beauties opening curl on curl, red ones so dark they seemed to turn black as they fell, and a certain exquisite cream kind with a slender red stem and bright scarlet leaves.

There were clumps of fairy bells, and all kinds of geraniums, and there were little trees of verbena and bluish lavender bushes and a bed of pelargoniums with velvet eyes and leaves like moths' wings. There was a bed of nothing but mignonette and another of nothing but pansies – borders of double and single daisies and all kinds of little tufty plants she had never seen before.

KATHERINE MANSFIELD

Paradise Discovered

A happy rural seat of various view;
  Groves whose rich trees wept odorous gums and balm,
Others whose fruit burnished with golden rind
  Hung amiable, Hesperian fables true,
If true, here only, and of delicious taste.
  Betwixt them lawns, or level downs, and flocks
Grazing the tender herb, were interposed,
  Or palmy hillock, or the flow'ry lap
Of some irriguous valley spread her store,
  Flow'rs of all hue, and without thorn the rose.
Another side, umbrageous grots and caves
  Of cool recess, o'er which the mantling vine
Lays forth her purple grape, and gently creeps
  Luxuriant; meanwhile murmuring waters fall
Down the slope hills, dispersed, or in a lake,
  That to the fringed bank with myrtle crowned
Her crystal mirror holds, unite their streams.
  The birds their quire apply; airs, vernal airs,
Breathing the smell of field and grove, attune
  The trembling leaves, while universal Pan,
Knit with the Graces and the Hours in dance,
  Led on th' eternal spring.

JOHN MILTON

The Devil's Plants

 SCARCELY DARE trust myself to speak of the weeds. They grow as if the devil was in them. I know a lady, a member of the church, and a very good sort of woman, considering the subject condition of that class, who says that the weeds work on her to that extent that, in going through her garden, she has the greatest difficulty in keeping the Ten Commandments in anything like an unfractured condition. I asked her which one? but she said all of them: one felt like breaking the whole lot. The sort of weed which I most hate (if I can be said to hate anything which grows in my garden) is the 'pusley,' a fat, ground-clinging, spreading, greasy thing, and the most propagatious (it is not my fault if the word is not in the dictionary) plant I know. I saw a Chinaman who came over with a returned missionary, and pretended to be converted, boil a lot of it in a pot, stir in eggs, and mix and eat it with relish – 'Me likee he'.... Who can say that other weeds which we despise may not be the favourite food of some remote people or tribe? It is possible that we destroy in our gardens that which is really of most value in some other place.

MARK TWAIN

LEPIDOPTERA. Papilio, Nimphalis.
HYMENOPTERA. Ichneumon.

Omar Khayyám's Retreat

With me along some Strip of Herbage strown,
That just divides the desert from the sown,
  Where name of Slave and Sultán scarce is known,
And pity Sultán Máhmúd on his Throne.

Here with a Loaf of Bread beneath the Bough,
A Flask of Wine, a Book of Verse – and Thou
  Beside me singing in the Wilderness –
And Wilderness is Paradise enow.

'How sweet is mortal sovreignty!' – think some:
Others – 'How blest the Paradise to come!'
  Ah, take the Cash in hand and waive the Rest;
Oh, the brave Music of a *distant* Drum!

Look to the Rose that blows about us – 'Lo,
'Laughing,' she says, 'into the World I blow:
  'At once the silken Tassel of my Purse
'Tear, and its Treasure on the Garden throw.'

EDWARD FITZGERALD

The Secret Garden

 HE MOVED away from the door, stepping as softly as if she were afraid of awakening someone. She was glad that there was grass under her feet and that her steps made no sounds. She walked under one of the fairy-like arches between the trees and looked up at the sprays and tendrils which formed them. 'I wonder if they are all quite dead,' she said. 'Is it all a quite dead garden? I wish it wasn't.'

But she was *inside* the wonderful garden, and she could come through the door under the ivy any time, and she felt as if she had found a world all her own. Everything was strange and silent, and she seemed to be hundreds of miles away from anyone, but somehow she did not feel lonely at all. All that troubled her was her wish that she knew whether all the roses were dead, or if perhaps some of them had lived and might put out leaves and buds as the weather got warmer.

FRANCES HODGSON BURNETT

A Gardener in Decline

THERE WAS ONE silent witness to the increasing decay of his powers that could not be overlooked. The garden gave him away. People coming to visit me and it were embarrassed to know what to say, or they even hinted that it would be an economy to allow Bettesworth a small pension and hire a younger man, who would do as much work, and do it better, in half the time. As if I needed to be told that! But then they were not witnesses, with me, of the pluck – better worth preserving than any garden – with which Bettesworth sought to make amends for his vanished youth. His tenacity deepened my regard for him, even while its poor results almost wore out my patience.... I could reconcile myself to indifferent crops, but exasperation was daily renewed by the little daily failures in routine work, owing to his defective sight, which grew worse and worse. There were the garden paths. With what care the old man drew his broom along them, working by faith and not sight, blindly feeling for the rubbish he could not see, and getting it all save from some corner or other of which his theories had forgotten to take account! Little nests of disorder collected in this way, to-day here, to-morrow somewhere else, surprising, offensive to the eye.

GEORGE BOURNE

A Poet's Advice on Horticulture

To build, to plant, whatever you intend,
    To rear the Column, or the Arch to bend,
To swell the Terras, or to sink the Grot;
    In all, let Nature never be forgot.
But treat the Goddess like a modest fair,
    Nor over-dress, nor leave her wholly bare;
Let not each beauty ev'ry where be spy'd,
    Where half the skill is decently to hide.
He gains all points, who pleasingly confounds,
    Surprizes, varies, and conceals the Bounds.
Consult the Genius of the Place in all;
    That tells the Waters or to rise, or fall,
Or helps th'ambitious Hill the heav'ns to scale,
    Or scoops in circling theatres the Vale;
Calls in the Country, catches op'ning glades,
    Joins willing woods, and varies shades from shades;
Now breaks, or now directs, th' intending Lines,
    Paints as you plant, and as you work, designs.

ALEXANDER POPE

Twilight Shadows

 N FINE WEATHER, the old gentleman is almost constantly in the garden; and, when it is too wet to go into it, he will look out of the window at it by the hour together. He has always something to do there, and you will see him digging, and sweeping, and cutting, and planting, with manifest delight. In spring time there is no end to the sowing of seeds, and sticking little bits of wood over them, with labels, which look like epitaphs to their memory.... On a summer's evening, when the large watering-pot has been filled and emptied some fourteen times, and the old couple have quite exhausted themselves by trotting about, you will see them sitting happily together in the little summer-house, enjoying the calm and peace of the twilight, and watching the shadows as they fall upon the garden, and, gradually growing thicker and more sombre, obscure the tints of their gayest flowers – no bad emblem of the years that have silently rolled over their heads, deadening in their course the brightest hues of early hopes and feelings which have long since faded away. These are their only recreations, and they require no more.

CHARLES DICKENS

Sources and Acknowledgments

For permission to reproduce illustrations, the publishers thank the following: Bridgeman Art Library, Sam Elder, Mary Evans Picture Library, E. T. Archive and the Mansell Collection.